Copyright © 2023 by Michael Jaynes (Author)

This book is protected by copyright law and is intended solely for personal use. Reproduction, distribution, or any other form of use requires the written permission of the author. The information presented in this book is for educational and entertainment purposes only, and while every effort has been made to ensure its accuracy and completeness, no guarantees are made. The author is not providing legal, financial, medical, or professional advice, and readers should consult with a licensed professional before implementing any of the techniques discussed in this book. The content in this book has been sourced from various reliable sources, but readers should exercise their own judgment when using this information. The author is not responsible for any losses, direct or indirect, that may occur from the use of this book, including but not limited to errors, omissions, or inaccuracies.

We hope this book has been informative and helpful on your journey to understanding and celebrating older adults. Thank you for your interest and support!

Title: Blood on the Field
Subtitle: The Ultimate Showdown in Sports

Series: Red War Rivalries: The Evolution and Impact of Sports' Greatest Feuds
By Michael Jaynes

"Liverpool against Manchester United is probably one of the most intense rivalries in football history."
Steven Gerrard, former Liverpool captain

"The rivalry between Liverpool and Manchester United is steeped in history, and it's something that every player wants to be a part of."
Rio Ferdinand, former Manchester United defender

"It's the greatest rivalry in sports, in my opinion. When you think about the history, the passion, the intensity, it's unmatched."
Alex Rodriguez, former Yankee player

"There's just something about playing the Yankees that brings out the best in the Red Sox, and vice versa. It's a special feeling."
Dustin Pedroia, former Red Sox player

"The Celtics-Lakers rivalry is the best in all of sports."
Bill Simmons

"It's always special when the Celtics and Lakers play. The history, the tradition, the excellence of both franchises, it's all there."
Larry Bird

"The McLaren-Ferrari rivalry was so intense because they were two of the biggest and most successful teams in Formula One history. They were always pushing each other to the limit, both on and off the track."
Martin Brundle, former Formula One driver and commentator

Table of Contents

Introduction 8

   The Intensity and Historical Significance of Red War Rivalries in Sports 8

   The Psychological and Emotional Impact of Rivalries on Athletes and Teams 11

   The Future of Red War Rivalries in Global Sports in the Age of Technology and Globalization 14

Chapter 1: Serena Williams vs. Maria Sharapova in Tennis . 17

   Origins of the Rivalry and How it Developed 17

   Key Matches and Memorable Moments that Shaped the Rivalry 19

   The Cultural Significance of the Rivalry in Tennis and Beyond 22

   Analysis of Their Playing Styles and How They Match Up Against Each Other 25

   Recent Matchups and Future Prospects for the Rivalry and Both Players 27

Chapter 2: Boston Celtics vs. Los Angeles Lakers in Basketball 29

   Origins of the Rivalry and How it Developed Over Time 29

   Key Players and Memorable Moments that Shaped the Rivalry 31

   The Impact of the Rivalry on the NBA and Basketball as a Whole 33

Analysis of the Teams' Playing Styles and How They Match Up Against Each Other 36

Recent Matchups and Future Prospects for the Rivalry and Both Teams 39

Chapter 3: Australia vs. England in Cricket 42

Origins of the Rivalry and How it Developed Over Time 42

Key Matches and Memorable Moments that Shaped the Rivalry 44

The Cultural Significance of the Rivalry in Cricket and Beyond 47

Analysis of the Teams' Playing Styles and How They Match Up Against Each Other 50

Recent Matchups and Future Prospects for the Rivalry and Both Teams 53

Chapter 4: Real Madrid vs. Barcelona in Soccer 56

Origins of the Rivalry and How it Developed Over Time 56

Key Players and Memorable Matches that Shaped the Rivalry 59

Cultural Significance of the Rivalry in Soccer and Beyond 62

Analysis of the Teams' Playing Styles and How They Match Up Against Each Other 65

Recent Matchups and Future Prospects for the Rivalry and Both Teams 68

Conclusion 73

Recap of the Importance and Significance of Red War Rivalries in Sports *73*

The Global Impact of Rivalries on Sports and Society *76*

The Future of Red War Rivalries in Sports in the Age of Technology and Globalization *79*

Lessons Learned from the Red War Rivalries and Their Impact on Athletes, Teams, and Fans *82*

Final Thoughts on the Future of Red War Rivalries in Sports . *85*

Key Terms and Definitions **87**

Supporting Materials **89**

Introduction
The Intensity and Historical Significance of Red War Rivalries in Sports

Red War rivalries in sports are some of the most intense and memorable competitions in athletic history. These rivalries often transcend the boundaries of sport and become cultural touchstones, with fans around the world following every match with bated breath.

What is it about these rivalries that makes them so compelling? One factor is certainly the high level of competition involved. Red War rivalries usually involve two teams or players that are evenly matched, both in terms of skill and in terms of the significance of the competition.

But there's also a historical aspect to these rivalries. Many of the most iconic Red War rivalries have been around for decades or even centuries, with each new match adding to the legacy of the rivalry. In this chapter, we'll take a closer look at the intensity and historical significance of Red War rivalries in sports, exploring some of the most famous and enduring rivalries in the world of athletics.

The Intensity of Red War Rivalries:

At the heart of any Red War rivalry is a fierce competitive spirit. Both teams or players want to come out on top, and the stakes are often high - whether it's a national championship, a major trophy, or just bragging rights. This intensity can manifest itself in a number of ways, from pre-game trash talk to physical confrontations on the field of play.

One example of this intensity is the Red War rivalry between Real Madrid and Barcelona in soccer. These two teams have been battling it out on the pitch since the early 20th century, with each new match adding to the tension between the two clubs. Fans of both teams are passionate and vocal, with emotions running high during each match.

Another example of intensity can be seen in the rivalry between Serena Williams and Maria Sharapova in tennis. These two players have been trading victories and barbs for years, with each match feeling like a high-stakes showdown. The intensity of their rivalry is further fueled by their contrasting playing styles and personalities, with Williams' power and aggression contrasting with Sharapova's precision and grace.

Historical Significance:

The historical significance of Red War rivalries can be seen in their lasting impact on sports and popular culture. These rivalries often transcend the boundaries of sport, becoming cultural touchstones that people around the world can identify with.

One example of this historical significance is the Red War rivalry between the Boston Celtics and the Los Angeles Lakers in basketball. These two teams have been battling it out on the court since the 1960s, with each new matchup adding to the legacy of the rivalry. The Celtics-Lakers rivalry has helped to define the NBA as a league, with each team representing a different style of play and a different approach to the game.

Another example of historical significance is the Red War rivalry between Australia and England in cricket. This rivalry dates back to the late 19th century, with each new match adding to the rich history of the competition. The cultural significance of this rivalry extends beyond the boundaries of sport, with each country's fans seeing the match as a chance to assert their national pride and identity.

Conclusion:

Red War rivalries in sports are intense, historic, and often transcend the boundaries of sport itself. These rivalries capture the imaginations of fans around the world, fueling their passion for their favorite teams and players. In the following chapters, we'll take a closer look at some of the most famous and enduring Red War rivalries in sports, exploring the key matches, players, and moments that have helped to define these legendary competitions.

The Psychological and Emotional Impact of Rivalries on Athletes and Teams

Sports rivalries are more than just matches between two teams or individuals. They represent a complex mix of history, culture, and emotions that transcend the game itself. Rivalries can ignite passions, create legends, and leave a lasting impact on athletes and fans alike. In this chapter, we will explore the psychological and emotional impact of rivalries on athletes and teams.

First, it is important to understand that rivalry is more than just competition. A rivalry is a special kind of competition that involves a history of past encounters, often characterized by tension, conflict, and animosity. The nature of the rivalry is shaped by the cultural, social, and historical context in which it occurs. For example, the rivalry between England and Australia in cricket is rooted in a history of colonization and a competition for dominance that extends beyond the boundaries of the game. Similarly, the rivalry between Real Madrid and Barcelona in soccer is intertwined with politics, regional identity, and national pride.

The psychological and emotional impact of rivalries on athletes and teams is multifaceted. At the individual level, athletes can experience a range of emotions, from excitement and motivation to anxiety and fear. The pressure to perform well and to win can be intense, and the emotional stakes can be high. In some cases, the intensity of the rivalry can lead to unsportsmanlike behavior, such as cheating or aggression. At the same time, rivalries can also bring out the best in athletes, inspiring them to push themselves beyond their limits and to achieve new heights of excellence.

At the team level, rivalries can create a sense of identity and belonging that goes beyond the game itself. Teams often define themselves in opposition to their rivals, and the intensity of the rivalry can serve as a rallying point for the team and its fans. This sense of identity and belonging can be a powerful motivator, driving athletes to perform at their best and to overcome adversity.

However, rivalries can also have negative consequences for athletes and teams. The pressure to win at all costs can lead to a culture of cheating, aggression, and unsportsmanlike behavior. In extreme cases, rivalries can lead to violence, both on and off the field. Moreover, the emotional toll of intense rivalries can take a toll on athletes, leading to burnout, anxiety, and other mental health issues.

In conclusion, the psychological and emotional impact of rivalries on athletes and teams is complex and multifaceted. Rivalries can bring out the best in athletes and inspire them to achieve new heights of excellence, but they can also create a culture of aggression and unsportsmanlike behavior. It is important for athletes, coaches, and fans to understand the emotional stakes of rivalries and to strive to promote healthy competition and sportsmanship both on and off the field.

The Future of Red War Rivalries in Global Sports in the Age of Technology and Globalization

As the world continues to become increasingly interconnected through technology and globalization, the landscape of sports is also evolving. Red War rivalries have been a part of sports for centuries, but how will these rivalries adapt and evolve in the face of these new changes? In this section, we will explore the future of Red War rivalries in global sports and the potential impact of technology and globalization on these rivalries.

Technology and Red War Rivalries

One of the most significant impacts of technology on sports has been the ability to connect fans from all over the world. Social media platforms such as Twitter and Instagram have given fans a way to connect with their favorite athletes and teams in real-time. This has created a new level of engagement between fans and athletes, and it has also given athletes and teams the ability to build their personal brand beyond the traditional limits of their sport.

As Red War rivalries continue to develop, the use of technology will likely become even more critical. Social media platforms may play a larger role in how athletes and teams communicate and interact with each other, and how fans engage with their favorite athletes and teams. For example, we may see more trash-talking and banter between rival athletes and teams on social media, adding a new level of intensity to these already fierce rivalries.

Globalization and Red War Rivalries

Globalization has had a significant impact on sports, as it has created opportunities for athletes and teams to compete on a global scale. However, globalization has also led to the homogenization of sports, as traditional rivalries may be diluted in favor of more international competitions.

Despite this, Red War rivalries are likely to continue to thrive in the age of globalization. As athletes and teams from different countries compete against each other, new rivalries may develop, and existing rivalries may take on a new level of intensity. This may be especially true in sports where certain countries or regions dominate, such as soccer or basketball.

The Impact of Technology and Globalization on Red War Rivalries

As technology and globalization continue to shape the sports landscape, the future of Red War rivalries is both exciting and uncertain. On the one hand, these new developments may provide new opportunities for athletes and teams to engage with each other and with fans, and may lead to the development of new rivalries. On the other hand, these new developments may also dilute traditional rivalries or change the way that athletes and teams interact with each other.

Ultimately, the future of Red War rivalries in global sports will be shaped by a combination of factors, including advances in technology, shifts in cultural and political dynamics, and changes in the global sports landscape. However, one thing is certain: Red War rivalries are likely to continue to play a significant role in sports, providing athletes and fans with an unparalleled level of excitement and intensity.

Chapter 1: Serena Williams vs. Maria Sharapova in Tennis

Origins of the Rivalry and How it Developed

The rivalry between Serena Williams and Maria Sharapova is one of the most intense and long-standing rivalries in women's tennis. It began in 2004 when the two players first met in the second round of the Miami Open. At that time, Serena was already a dominant force in the game, having won six Grand Slam singles titles, while Sharapova was still an up-and-coming player, just 17 years old.

Their first encounter was a close match, with Serena winning 6-4, 6-3. However, it was what happened after the match that set the stage for the rivalry to develop. In her post-match press conference, Sharapova made a comment about Serena's rumored relationship with a male player, which was widely interpreted as a dig at Serena's personal life. Serena was clearly angry about the comment and fired back with some pointed remarks of her own.

From that point on, the rivalry between Serena and Sharapova only intensified. They met many times over the years, including in four Grand Slam finals, with Serena winning all four. The matches were often highly competitive and filled with drama, with both players pushing each other to the limit.

Part of what made the rivalry so intense was the contrast between the two players. Serena was known for her power and athleticism, while Sharapova was known for her precision and mental toughness. Their different styles of play and personalities made for a compelling matchup, and fans and commentators alike were often drawn into the drama.

Off the court, the rivalry also played out in the media, with both players making pointed comments about each other in interviews and press conferences. Sharapova, in particular, was known for her willingness to speak her mind, and her comments about Serena often fueled the fire of the rivalry.

Overall, the rivalry between Serena Williams and Maria Sharapova is one of the most storied and dramatic in the history of tennis. Its origins can be traced back to a single match in 2004, but the intense competition, drama, and off-court controversies that followed helped to make it one of the defining rivalries of the sport.

Key Matches and Memorable Moments that Shaped the Rivalry

The rivalry between Serena Williams and Maria Sharapova has produced some of the most memorable moments in modern tennis history. From Grand Slam finals to Olympic matchups, the two players have faced off in high-pressure situations on numerous occasions, each match adding to the intensity of their rivalry. Here are some of the key matches and memorable moments that have shaped their rivalry.

1. Wimbledon Final, 2004 The 2004 Wimbledon final was the first Grand Slam final between Serena and Maria, and it was a match that Sharapova would never forget. Despite being the underdog, Sharapova put in an impressive performance, winning the first set and holding her own against Williams. However, Williams would eventually come out on top, winning the match in straight sets. The match set the tone for the rivalry, with Sharapova determined to prove herself against the dominant Williams.

2. Australian Open Final, 2007 In the 2007 Australian Open final, Williams and Sharapova met again, and once again, Williams came out on top. However, the match was not without controversy, as Sharapova accused Williams of trying to distract her during the match. Williams was

reportedly making loud grunting noises during Sharapova's serve, leading to accusations of gamesmanship. The incident only added fuel to the fire of their rivalry.

3. Olympic Gold Medal Match, 2012 The London Olympics in 2012 saw Williams and Sharapova go head-to-head once again, this time in the gold medal match. The match was a one-sided affair, with Williams dominating Sharapova to win the gold medal in straight sets. The victory was particularly sweet for Williams, as Sharapova had carried the Russian flag in the opening ceremony of the games, leading to a great deal of media attention and hype around their matchup.

4. Wimbledon Final, 2015 The 2015 Wimbledon final was the most recent Grand Slam final between Williams and Sharapova, and it was a match that lived up to the hype. With both players in top form, the match was an intense back-and-forth battle, with Williams eventually coming out on top in three sets. The victory marked Williams' 21st Grand Slam title, cementing her status as one of the greatest tennis players of all time.

5. Off-Court Drama In addition to their on-court battles, Williams and Sharapova have also had their fair share of off-court drama, including a long-running feud that has played out in the media. Sharapova has been critical of

Williams' behavior in the past, accusing her of being disrespectful and unprofessional. Williams, in turn, has been dismissive of Sharapova's complaints, and the two have traded barbs in interviews and on social media. The drama only adds to the intensity of their rivalry, keeping fans and media outlets alike interested in their ongoing battles.

Overall, the key matches and memorable moments that have shaped the rivalry between Serena Williams and Maria Sharapova have been some of the most exciting and dramatic in modern tennis history. With each new matchup, the tension between the two players only seems to grow, and fans can't wait to see what the future holds for this intense and captivating rivalry.

The Cultural Significance of the Rivalry in Tennis and Beyond

The rivalry between Serena Williams and Maria Sharapova in tennis has had a significant cultural impact on the sport and beyond. This chapter explores the cultural significance of the rivalry and how it has shaped perceptions of women in sports and society as a whole.

At its core, the Williams vs. Sharapova rivalry represents a clash of cultures. Williams, a Black woman from Compton, California, and Sharapova, a white woman from Russia, come from vastly different backgrounds and embody different ideals of femininity and athleticism. Their rivalry has sparked conversations about race, class, and gender in the sport of tennis and beyond.

One of the most memorable moments in the rivalry came in 2018 when Williams defeated Sharapova in the first round of the French Open. It was Williams' first major tournament since giving birth to her daughter and Sharapova's first Grand Slam match in over a year due to a doping suspension. The match was highly anticipated, but it was Williams' outfit that stole the show. She wore a black catsuit that she said made her feel like a "warrior princess." The outfit drew both admiration and criticism, with some arguing that it was inappropriate for the sport.

The cultural impact of the Williams vs. Sharapova rivalry can also be seen in the way that it has influenced the wider conversation about women in sports. Williams, in particular, has been a vocal advocate for gender equality in tennis and beyond. In 2019, she penned an essay for Harper's Bazaar in which she discussed the double standards that women face in sports and society. She wrote, "We must continue to dream big, and in doing so, we empower the next generation of women to be just as bold in their pursuits."

The impact of the rivalry extends beyond tennis as well. Williams and Sharapova are both highly visible figures in popular culture, and their rivalry has helped to shape the way that women in sports are perceived by the broader public. Their contrasting styles and backgrounds have made them emblematic of different visions of femininity and athleticism, and their rivalry has sparked conversations about what it means to be a successful female athlete.

In conclusion, the cultural significance of the Williams vs. Sharapova rivalry in tennis cannot be overstated. The clash of cultures and personalities has made the rivalry one of the most compelling in sports history, and its impact extends far beyond the court. Through their words and actions, Williams and Sharapova have helped to shape the conversation about gender and race in sports and society as a whole.

Analysis of Their Playing Styles and How They Match Up Against Each Other

Serena Williams and Maria Sharapova are two of the greatest tennis players of all time, and their rivalry on the court has been one of the most intense and high-profile in the history of the sport. In this chapter, we will analyze their playing styles and how they match up against each other.

Serena Williams is known for her powerful serve and aggressive baseline play. She has a strong and consistent backhand and forehand, and she uses her athleticism and speed to cover the court effectively. Williams also has a competitive edge and mental toughness that allows her to perform well under pressure.

Maria Sharapova, on the other hand, is known for her precision and technique. She has a strong serve and a consistent groundstroke game, with a particular emphasis on her backhand. Sharapova is also known for her focus and determination on the court, which has helped her to overcome injuries and setbacks throughout her career.

When these two players face off against each other, their contrasting styles of play create a fascinating matchup. Williams' power and aggression can overwhelm Sharapova's precision and technique, but Sharapova's focus and determination can help her to stay in rallies and force Williams to make errors.

In terms of their head-to-head record, Williams has a dominant record against Sharapova, with 20 wins to Sharapova's 2. This is in part due to Williams' superior athleticism and power, which have allowed her to dictate play and control the outcome of their matches.

However, Sharapova has had some notable victories over Williams, including a win in the 2004 Wimbledon final, which was her first Grand Slam title. Sharapova has also been able to push Williams to three sets in some of their matches, demonstrating her ability to compete at a high level against one of the greatest players of all time.

Looking ahead, it will be interesting to see how their rivalry evolves as both players continue to compete at the highest level. Williams is now in the later stages of her career, while Sharapova has retired from professional tennis. However, their legacy as two of the greatest players in the history of the sport, and their intense rivalry, will continue to be remembered and celebrated by tennis fans around the world.

Recent Matchups and Future Prospects for the Rivalry and Both Players

Serena Williams and Maria Sharapova have faced off against each other 22 times in their professional careers, with Serena holding a dominant 20-2 record. However, despite the lopsided record, the rivalry between the two players remains one of the most talked-about in tennis.

In recent years, the rivalry has lost some of its intensity due to a lack of competitive matches. Sharapova retired from professional tennis in 2020, leaving fans without the prospect of any more matches between the two players. However, the rivalry remains a topic of discussion among tennis fans and experts.

Recent Matchups:

The most recent meeting between Williams and Sharapova took place at the 2019 US Open, where Williams won in straight sets in the first round. Prior to that, the two players had not faced each other since the 2016 Australian Open quarterfinals, where Williams once again won in straight sets.

In fact, Williams has won their last 18 matches dating back to 2005, with Sharapova's last victory coming at the 2004 WTA Tour Championships.

Future Prospects:

With Sharapova now retired from professional tennis, the prospect of any future matches between the two players seems unlikely. However, the impact of their rivalry on the sport of tennis is sure to be felt for years to come.

Both Williams and Sharapova have left an indelible mark on the sport, with Williams currently holding 23 Grand Slam singles titles and Sharapova having won five. The two players also served as role models and inspirations for countless young girls around the world who dream of playing professional tennis.

While their rivalry may have come to an end, their impact on the sport of tennis and the athletes who come after them will be felt for generations to come.

Chapter 2: Boston Celtics vs. Los Angeles Lakers in Basketball

Origins of the Rivalry and How it Developed Over Time

The rivalry between the Boston Celtics and Los Angeles Lakers is one of the most storied in all of sports, with roots dating back to the 1950s. Understanding the origins of the rivalry and how it developed over time can provide important context for its significance in the world of basketball and beyond.

The Boston Celtics were founded in 1946 and were the first franchise to establish a true dynasty in the NBA. Led by Bill Russell, the Celtics won eleven championships between 1957 and 1969, cementing their place in basketball history. Meanwhile, the Los Angeles Lakers were founded in 1947 and emerged as a powerhouse in the 1970s, led by legendary center Kareem Abdul-Jabbar and guard Magic Johnson.

The first meeting between the Celtics and Lakers in the NBA Finals came in 1959, with Boston winning the series 4-0. The two teams would meet again in the Finals in 1962, 1963, and 1965, with Boston winning each time. These early matchups laid the groundwork for what would become a fierce rivalry.

In the 1980s, the rivalry reached new heights with the emergence of Larry Bird for the Celtics and Magic Johnson for the Lakers. The two superstars faced off in the NBA Finals three times, with each team winning once before the Lakers took the decisive matchup in 1987. These matchups captured the attention of basketball fans around the world and helped to establish the NBA as a major professional sports league.

The rivalry continued into the 21st century, with the Celtics and Lakers meeting in the NBA Finals twice in three years in 2008 and 2010. Led by Paul Pierce and Kevin Garnett, the Celtics took the first matchup in six games, while Kobe Bryant and Pau Gasol led the Lakers to victory in the second matchup in seven games.

The origins of the rivalry between the Celtics and Lakers can be traced back to the early days of the NBA and the teams' respective successes on the court. The fierce competition between the two franchises over the years has only served to deepen the animosity and make for some of the most exciting basketball matchups in history.

Key Players and Memorable Moments that Shaped the Rivalry

The rivalry between the Boston Celtics and the Los Angeles Lakers is one of the most famous and intense rivalries in the history of professional basketball. Over the years, there have been many key players and memorable moments that have shaped this rivalry into what it is today.

One of the key players in the Celtics-Lakers rivalry is Larry Bird. Bird was a dominant force on the court and helped lead the Celtics to three championships in the 1980s. His rivalry with Magic Johnson, the star player for the Lakers, is one of the most famous in sports history. The two players were so closely linked that they were often referred to as the "Bird-Magic" rivalry.

Another key player in the rivalry is Kobe Bryant. Bryant played for the Lakers from 1996 to 2016 and helped lead the team to five championships. He had many memorable matchups against the Celtics, including the 2010 NBA Finals, which the Lakers won in seven games.

In terms of memorable moments, there have been many that have helped shape this rivalry over the years. One of the most famous is the 1984 NBA Finals, which featured the Celtics and the Lakers. The series was tied at 2-2 heading into Game 5, which was played in Boston. With the game tied in the closing seconds, Bird stole an inbound pass from the Lakers and passed it to Dennis Johnson, who hit the game-winning layup. The Celtics went on to win the championship that year.

Another memorable moment came in the 2008 NBA Finals, which once again featured the Celtics and the Lakers. The Celtics won the championship that year, thanks in part to a dominant performance by Paul Pierce in Game 6. Pierce scored 17 of his 39 points in the third quarter and helped lead the Celtics to a 131-92 victory.

Throughout the years, there have been many other memorable moments in the Celtics-Lakers rivalry, from dramatic buzzer-beaters to heated confrontations between players. Each of these moments has helped to build the intensity and passion of this long-standing rivalry.

Overall, the Celtics-Lakers rivalry has been shaped by many key players and memorable moments over the years. From Larry Bird to Kobe Bryant, and from the 1984 NBA Finals to the 2008 NBA Finals, this rivalry has become an integral part of the history of professional basketball.

The Impact of the Rivalry on the NBA and Basketball as a Whole

The rivalry between the Boston Celtics and the Los Angeles Lakers has had a significant impact on the NBA and basketball as a whole. From their first meeting in the 1959 NBA Finals to their most recent matchups, the Celtics-Lakers rivalry has captured the attention of fans and the media alike. In this chapter, we will examine the impact of this rivalry on the NBA and basketball as a whole.

The Celtics-Lakers rivalry is often seen as a symbol of the East-West divide in the NBA. The Celtics, from the Eastern Conference, were seen as a team that played with grit, determination, and team spirit. The Lakers, from the Western Conference, were seen as a team that played with style, flair, and individual talent. This rivalry helped to popularize the NBA on a national level, as fans across the country picked a side in the rivalry and tuned in to watch these two teams battle it out on the court.

One of the key impacts of the rivalry was the way it transformed the NBA Finals. The Celtics and Lakers have met in the NBA Finals a total of 12 times, with the Lakers winning nine of those matchups. The intensity of these Finals series helped to establish the NBA as a premier sports league in the United States. Fans eagerly awaited the matchup between the Celtics and Lakers each year, and the NBA capitalized on this by promoting the rivalry through marketing and media coverage.

The Celtics-Lakers rivalry also helped to elevate individual players to legendary status. Players like Bill Russell, Larry Bird, Magic Johnson, and Kobe Bryant all played key roles in the rivalry, and their performances in Celtics-Lakers matchups helped to solidify their legacies. These players were able to rise to the occasion and perform at their best in the high-pressure environment of the rivalry, earning the respect and admiration of fans and fellow players alike.

Another impact of the rivalry was the way it helped to shape the NBA's competitive landscape. The Celtics and Lakers have a combined 34 NBA championships, with both teams consistently fielding talented rosters throughout their history. The rivalry pushed both teams to improve and innovate in order to gain an edge over their opponent. This led to the development of new playing styles, offensive and defensive strategies, and training techniques that have had a lasting impact on the NBA.

Finally, the rivalry between the Celtics and Lakers helped to raise the profile of basketball as a global sport. The rivalry attracted fans from around the world, and helped to establish the NBA as a truly international league. Players from all over the world have been inspired by the performances of Celtics and Lakers players in the rivalry, and have gone on to make their mark in the NBA.

In conclusion, the impact of the Celtics-Lakers rivalry on the NBA and basketball as a whole cannot be overstated. This rivalry helped to popularize the NBA on a national and global level, transformed the NBA Finals into a premier sports event, elevated individual players to legendary status, helped to shape the NBA's competitive landscape, and inspired players from around the world. The Celtics-Lakers rivalry is a testament to the power of sports to capture the imagination of fans and leave a lasting impact on the world.

Analysis of the Teams' Playing Styles and How They Match Up Against Each Other

The rivalry between the Boston Celtics and the Los Angeles Lakers has produced some of the greatest moments in basketball history. It is a classic matchup between two of the most successful teams in the NBA, and their styles of play have always been very different.

The Celtics have always been known for their strong defense, physical play, and teamwork. Their players are disciplined, and they work together as a unit to control the game. The Celtics are also known for their strong post play, with players like Bill Russell and Kevin McHale dominating in the paint. The team has a tradition of playing tough, hard-nosed basketball that has earned them many victories over the years.

On the other hand, the Lakers have always been known for their high-scoring offense and flashy style of play. The team has produced some of the most exciting players in the game, including Magic Johnson, Kobe Bryant, and Shaquille O'Neal. The Lakers rely on their individual talent and creativity to win games, and they often dominate their opponents with their fast-paced, up-tempo style of play.

When these two teams face off, it is always a clash of styles. The Celtics try to slow down the game and control the tempo, while the Lakers try to speed things up and create fast break opportunities. This dynamic has produced many memorable moments over the years, as both teams have pushed each other to their limits.

One of the most famous matchups between these two teams was in the 1984 NBA Finals. The Celtics, led by Larry Bird, were facing the Lakers, led by Magic Johnson. The series went to seven games, and in the final game, Bird put on a masterful performance, scoring 20 points and grabbing 12 rebounds to lead the Celtics to victory.

Another memorable matchup was in the 2010 NBA Finals, when the Lakers, led by Kobe Bryant, faced off against the Celtics, led by Paul Pierce. The series was once again a battle of contrasting styles, with the Lakers' offense going up against the Celtics' defense. In the end, it was the Lakers who emerged victorious, winning the series in seven games.

Despite the differences in their playing styles, both teams have had great success over the years. The Celtics have won a total of 17 NBA championships, while the Lakers have won 16. Their rivalry has played a significant role in the development of the NBA, and it has helped to make basketball one of the most popular sports in the world.

In conclusion, the matchup between the Boston Celtics and the Los Angeles Lakers is one of the greatest rivalries in sports history. Their contrasting styles of play have produced many memorable moments, and their impact on the NBA has been significant. As long as these two teams continue to play, their rivalry will remain a highlight of the NBA season.

Recent Matchups and Future Prospects for the Rivalry and Both Teams

The Boston Celtics vs. Los Angeles Lakers rivalry has been one of the most iconic rivalries in the history of sports. As both teams have a long-standing history of excellence, their matches are always highly anticipated, and the competition is intense. In this section, we will analyze the recent matchups between the two teams and discuss the future prospects of the rivalry and both teams.

Recent Matchups:

In recent years, the Boston Celtics and Los Angeles Lakers have played each other several times. In the 2019-2020 NBA season, the two teams faced each other twice in the regular season. The first match was held on January 20, 2020, at the TD Garden in Boston, where the Celtics beat the Lakers 139-107. The second match was held on February 23, 2020, at the Staples Center in Los Angeles, where the Lakers beat the Celtics 114-112.

The 2020-2021 season saw the two teams face each other twice again in the regular season. The first match was held on January 30, 2021, at the TD Garden in Boston, where the Lakers beat the Celtics 96-95. The second match was held on April 15, 2021, at the Staples Center in Los Angeles, where the Celtics beat the Lakers 121-113.

Future Prospects:

Both teams have been going through some changes, with new players coming in and old players retiring or leaving the team. For the Boston Celtics, Jayson Tatum and Jaylen Brown have emerged as key players and have been instrumental in the team's recent success. The team has also acquired players such as Evan Fournier, who is expected to strengthen their offense.

For the Los Angeles Lakers, LeBron James and Anthony Davis continue to be the driving force of the team. However, injuries and a lack of depth have been a concern for the team. The Lakers have made some moves in the offseason, acquiring players such as Russell Westbrook, who is expected to bring a new dimension to the team's offense.

As both teams continue to make changes to their rosters, it will be interesting to see how they match up against each other in the future. The rivalry between the Celtics and Lakers is expected to continue to be a highlight of the NBA season, and fans can look forward to some exciting matches in the years to come.

Conclusion:

The Boston Celtics vs. Los Angeles Lakers rivalry is one of the greatest rivalries in the history of sports. The rivalry has been shaped by some of the greatest players in the game, memorable moments, and a long-standing history of excellence. In recent years, the two teams have continued to face each other, and the competition has remained intense.

As both teams continue to evolve, the future prospects for the rivalry and both teams look bright. The Boston Celtics and Los Angeles Lakers are both expected to continue to be contenders in the NBA, and fans can look forward to some exciting matchups in the future.

Chapter 3: Australia vs. England in Cricket Origins of the Rivalry and How it Developed Over Time

The rivalry between Australia and England in cricket has a long and storied history, dating back to the 19th century. The origins of the rivalry can be traced back to the colonial era, when Australia was still a British colony and the game of cricket was seen as a means of asserting English superiority over their Australian counterparts.

The first official Test match between the two countries took place in Melbourne in 1877, marking the beginning of what would become one of the greatest rivalries in cricket history. Over the next few decades, the two countries would compete fiercely on the cricket field, with each team seeking to establish dominance over the other.

One of the key factors that contributed to the development of the Australia-England cricket rivalry was the competitive nature of the two nations. Both countries have a strong sporting culture, and cricket has always been a sport that has held a special place in the hearts of fans in both countries. This competitiveness spilled over onto the cricket field, with players from both teams determined to come out on top.

Another factor that contributed to the development of the rivalry was the social and political context in which it developed. During the early years of the rivalry, Australia was still a British colony, and there was a sense among some Australians that they were being treated as second-class citizens by their British counterparts. This sense of resentment towards the British spilled over into the cricket field, with Australian players often looking to beat England as a means of asserting their own national identity.

The rivalry between Australia and England has also been shaped by some of the key personalities involved in the game. Over the years, there have been many great players from both countries who have contributed to the intensity of the rivalry, including legends like Don Bradman, Ian Botham, Shane Warne, and Andrew Flintoff.

Overall, the Australia-England cricket rivalry is one of the oldest and most intense rivalries in the history of the sport. Its origins can be traced back to the colonial era, but it has been shaped by a variety of factors, including the competitive nature of the two nations, the social and political context in which it developed, and the personalities involved in the game. Despite the passage of time, the rivalry remains as strong as ever, with both countries continuing to compete fiercely on the cricket field.

Key Matches and Memorable Moments that Shaped the Rivalry

Australia and England have a long and storied cricketing rivalry, dating back over a century. Here are some of the key matches and moments that have shaped this intense and historic rivalry:

1. The Ashes Series of 1882: This series is considered the birthplace of the Ashes, the iconic trophy that is contested between the two nations. England lost the match at the Oval, and a satirical obituary in the Sporting Times declared that English cricket had died, and the ashes taken to Australia. This started a tradition that continues to this day, with the Ashes being one of the most hotly contested trophies in cricket.

2. The Bodyline Series of 1932-33: This series was marked by the use of the controversial Bodyline tactic by the English bowlers, which involved bowling short deliveries aimed at the body of the batsman. This tactic was designed to combat the dominance of Australian batsman Don Bradman, who was widely considered to be the greatest batsman of his time. The series was marked by acrimony and controversy, with the Australian team accusing the English of unsporting behaviour.

3. The tied Test of 1960: The second Test of the 1960-61 series in Brisbane was one of the most thrilling matches in cricketing history. Australia and England were evenly matched throughout the match, and the scores were tied at the end of the fifth day. This was only the second tied Test in history, and it remains one of the most memorable moments in the rivalry.

4. The Centenary Test of 1977: The Centenary Test, played at the Melbourne Cricket Ground in 1977, was held to commemorate the 100th anniversary of the first Test match between the two nations. The match was fiercely contested, and Australia won by 45 runs. The match was notable for a century by Dennis Lillee, who also took six wickets in the second innings.

5. The 2005 Ashes Series: The 2005 Ashes series is considered by many to be the greatest Test series of all time. England won the series 2-1, their first Ashes victory in 18 years. The series was marked by some of the most dramatic and thrilling cricket ever played, with both sides displaying great skill and determination.

These are just a few of the key matches and moments that have shaped the Australia vs. England cricketing rivalry. The intense competition and fierce rivalry between the two nations have made for some of the most memorable moments in cricketing history.

The Cultural Significance of the Rivalry in Cricket and Beyond

The Ashes, the name given to the Test cricket series between Australia and England, is considered one of the most iconic and prestigious sporting events in the world. The rivalry between Australia and England in cricket has a cultural significance that extends beyond the sport itself, with a long and complex history that reflects the relationship between the two countries.

The first recorded cricket match between Australia and England took place in 1861, but it was not until the 1880s that the rivalry began to take shape. In 1882, Australia won a Test match against England on English soil for the first time, which prompted The Sporting Times newspaper to publish a satirical obituary for English cricket, stating that its "body will be cremated and the ashes taken to Australia." Thus, the Ashes were born, and the rivalry between Australia and England in cricket took on a new level of intensity.

The cultural significance of the Ashes is evident in the way it has been commemorated and celebrated over the years. For instance, in the lead-up to each series, the English and Australian media engage in a war of words, with each country seeking to gain a psychological edge over the other. The series itself is often accompanied by elaborate pre-match ceremonies, such as the singing of the national anthems and the presentation of the Ashes urn to the winning team.

The rivalry has also had a profound impact on the way cricket is played and perceived in both countries. In Australia, cricket is seen as a quintessentially Australian sport, and success against England is considered a matter of national pride. Similarly, in England, cricket is seen as a symbol of Englishness, and a victory against Australia is considered a triumph over a former colonial power.

Outside of cricket, the rivalry has also had an impact on the broader cultural relationship between Australia and England. The Ashes are often used as a metaphor for the historical and cultural tensions between the two countries, with each side seeking to assert its superiority over the other.

In recent years, however, the cultural significance of the rivalry has become somewhat diluted by the rise of globalisation and the increasing professionalisation of cricket. The Ashes are now just one of many international cricket series played each year, and the rivalry between Australia and England is no longer the only focus of attention for cricket fans around the world.

Despite this, the Ashes remain an important and iconic sporting event, and the rivalry between Australia and England in cricket continues to captivate fans and players alike. The cultural significance of the rivalry may have evolved over time, but its legacy remains an important part of the sporting and cultural heritage of both countries.

Analysis of the Teams' Playing Styles and How They Match Up Against Each Other

Introduction: The rivalry between Australia and England in cricket is one of the most intense and long-standing rivalries in sports. The two countries have been competing against each other in the sport since the late 19th century, and the rivalry has only grown stronger over time. In this chapter, we will analyze the playing styles of both teams and how they match up against each other.

The Teams' Playing Styles: Australia and England have very different playing styles when it comes to cricket. Australia is known for its aggressive, attacking style of play, while England tends to be more defensive and cautious. Australia relies heavily on its fast bowlers, who are known for their pace, swing, and accuracy. The Australian team also has some of the best batsmen in the world, who are equally comfortable playing both pace and spin bowling.

On the other hand, England is known for its strong and disciplined bowling attack, led by James Anderson and Stuart Broad. England's batting line-up is also solid, with players like Joe Root and Jonny Bairstow capable of scoring big runs. However, England tends to play a more cautious style of cricket, relying on their bowlers to take wickets and restrict the opposition's scoring.

How They Match Up Against Each Other: When Australia and England face each other on the cricket field, it is always a highly anticipated and closely watched match. Both teams have a long history of fierce competition, and the intensity of the rivalry is palpable.

One of the key factors in how the two teams match up against each other is the conditions in which they are playing. In Australia, where the pitches are faster and bouncier, the Australian team tends to have the advantage due to their strong pace bowling attack. However, in England, where the pitches are slower and more conducive to swing bowling, the advantage tends to swing towards the English team.

Another factor that comes into play is the mental aspect of the game. Both teams are known for their competitive spirit and never-say-die attitude, and this often comes into play in close matches. The team that can stay calm under pressure and make the right decisions in critical moments is often the one that comes out on top.

Recent Matchups and Future Prospects for the Rivalry: In recent years, Australia and England have played each other in some highly entertaining and closely contested matches. The 2019 Ashes series, in particular, was a thrilling back-and-forth affair that saw the two teams battle it out for the trophy.

Looking ahead, the future of the Australia-England rivalry in cricket looks bright. Both teams have a new generation of young players coming through the ranks, who will be eager to make their mark on the international stage. With both teams having a strong core of experienced players as well, the stage is set for some exciting contests in the years to come.

Conclusion: The rivalry between Australia and England in cricket is one that has stood the test of time. The two teams have a rich history of fierce competition, and their playing styles and strategies have evolved over the years. As we have seen, the key to success in this rivalry often comes down to mental strength and the ability to perform under pressure. With both teams having a strong core of players and a bright future ahead, the Australia-England rivalry looks set to continue to capture the imagination of cricket fans around the world.

Recent Matchups and Future Prospects for the Rivalry and Both Teams

Australia and England continue to face each other in cricket matches around the world, with each match adding to the long-standing rivalry between the two nations. In recent years, both teams have had their ups and downs, and their performances against each other have reflected this.

In the last decade, Australia and England have played a number of thrilling matches, including some nail-biting finishes that have gone down to the wire. One such match was the third Test of the 2019 Ashes series, played at Headingley in Leeds. England were chasing 359 runs in the fourth innings and were struggling at 286-9 when Ben Stokes played one of the greatest innings in Test history to secure a one-wicket win for England.

In the same series, Australia retained the Ashes for the first time in 18 years, after a 2-2 draw in the five-match series. Steve Smith was the standout player of the series, scoring an incredible 774 runs in just seven innings, including three centuries and three fifties.

More recently, in the 2020-21 season, Australia beat England 2-1 in a three-match ODI series, with the last two matches being played at Old Trafford in Manchester. Australia won the first match comfortably, by 19 runs, thanks to a brilliant century by Glenn Maxwell. England bounced back to win the second match by 24 runs, but Australia took the series by winning the third match by three wickets, with just two balls to spare.

Looking ahead, both Australia and England have a number of young and talented players who are looking to establish themselves in the international arena. For Australia, the likes of Marnus Labuschagne, Cameron Green, and Will Pucovski are exciting prospects who have already shown their potential. England, on the other hand, have the likes of Zak Crawley, Ollie Pope, and Dom Sibley, who have all shown glimpses of their talent.

The two teams are set to play a number of high-profile matches in the coming years, including the 2021-22 Ashes series in Australia, which will be a crucial test for both teams. Australia will be looking to build on their recent success in England and win back-to-back Ashes series, while England will be hoping to bounce back and regain the Ashes on Australian soil.

In addition to the Ashes, both teams will also be playing in the upcoming ICC T20 World Cup, which will be held in India in 2021. This tournament will be a great opportunity for both teams to showcase their skills and compete against the best T20 teams in the world.

In conclusion, the rivalry between Australia and England in cricket is one of the oldest and most storied in the history of the sport. The two teams have played some of the greatest matches in cricket history, and their performances against each other continue to captivate fans around the world. With a number of young and talented players on both sides, the future of the rivalry looks bright, and fans can look forward to many more thrilling matches between these two great cricketing nations.

Chapter 4: Real Madrid vs. Barcelona in Soccer Origins of the Rivalry and How it Developed Over Time

Real Madrid and Barcelona, two of the world's most iconic football clubs, have been fierce rivals for over 100 years. The rivalry, known as El Clásico, is steeped in history and is a staple of the football calendar. In this chapter, we will explore the origins of the Real Madrid vs. Barcelona rivalry and how it developed over time.

Origins of the Rivalry The roots of the rivalry between Real Madrid and Barcelona can be traced back to the early 20th century. Football was gaining popularity in Spain, and both clubs were founded in the same decade. Real Madrid was founded in 1902, while Barcelona was founded in 1899.

The political landscape of Spain at the time was also a factor in the development of the rivalry. Barcelona, the capital of Catalonia, had a distinct culture and language that differed from the rest of Spain. Real Madrid, on the other hand, was seen as a symbol of the central government and the Spanish monarchy.

The first meeting between the two clubs took place in 1902, just a few months after Real Madrid's founding. Barcelona won the game 3-1, but the rivalry did not truly start until the 1920s. During this time, Barcelona became the first club to win the Spanish Cup, while Real Madrid won their first league title in 1932.

The rivalry intensified in the 1940s and 1950s when Francisco Franco came to power in Spain. Franco was a fan of Real Madrid, and the club became known as the "team of the regime." Barcelona, on the other hand, was seen as a symbol of Catalan identity and was often persecuted by the regime.

The rivalry continued to grow in the 1960s and 1970s as both clubs experienced success on the European stage. Real Madrid won the first five European Cups, while Barcelona won their first in 1992.

How the Rivalry Developed Over Time The Real Madrid vs. Barcelona rivalry has continued to evolve over the years. One of the biggest factors in the rivalry's development has been the success of the two clubs. Both Real Madrid and Barcelona have been among the most successful clubs in Europe and the world.

Another factor has been the rise of individual players. Players such as Alfredo Di Stefano, Ferenc Puskas, Johan Cruyff, Lionel Messi, and Cristiano Ronaldo have all played a significant role in the rivalry's development. These players have been instrumental in shaping the style and success of their respective clubs.

Off the field, the rivalry has also been shaped by the personalities of the two clubs' presidents. Santiago Bernabeu, who served as Real Madrid's president from 1943 to 1978, was a visionary who transformed the club into a global brand. Joan Laporta, who served as Barcelona's president from 2003 to 2010, was a charismatic leader who helped modernize the club.

The rivalry has also been shaped by political and cultural factors. The debate over Catalan independence has been a hot topic in Spain for decades, and Barcelona's identity as a Catalan club has played a role in the rivalry. Additionally, the rivalry has been influenced by the clubs' different playing styles. Real Madrid is known for its attacking football, while Barcelona is known for its possession-based game.

Conclusion The Real Madrid vs. Barcelona rivalry is one of the oldest and most storied rivalries in football. The rivalry has been shaped by a variety of factors, including politics, culture, and individual players. While the rivalry has had its ups and downs over the years, it remains one of the most intense and exciting rivalries in world football.

Key Players and Memorable Matches that Shaped the Rivalry

The rivalry between Real Madrid and Barcelona, also known as "El Clásico," has seen some of the greatest footballers in history compete against each other. From the legendary Alfredo Di Stefano and Ferenc Puskas to Lionel Messi and Cristiano Ronaldo, the rivalry has produced some of the most iconic players of all time. In this section, we will look at the key players and memorable matches that have shaped the Real Madrid-Barcelona rivalry.

Alfredo Di Stefano Arguably one of the greatest footballers of all time, Alfredo Di Stefano played for Real Madrid between 1953 and 1964. He played a crucial role in the club's domination of European football during that period, winning five European Cups in a row between 1956 and 1960. Di Stefano also played a significant role in the Real Madrid-Barcelona rivalry, scoring many important goals against Barcelona, including the winner in the 1960 European Cup final.

Ferenc Puskas Ferenc Puskas joined Real Madrid in 1958 and went on to form a lethal partnership with Di Stefano. Puskas was known for his incredible left foot and his ability to score goals from almost any position on the field. He played a crucial role in Real Madrid's domination of

European football in the late 1950s and early 1960s, winning three European Cups in a row between 1959 and 1961. Puskas also played a key role in the Real Madrid-Barcelona rivalry, scoring many important goals against Barcelona.

Lionel Messi Lionel Messi is undoubtedly one of the greatest footballers of all time, and his performances in El Clásico have been nothing short of spectacular. Messi made his Barcelona debut in 2004 and has since gone on to score 26 goals in El Clásico, making him the all-time top scorer in the fixture. Messi has been a key player in Barcelona's recent dominance over Real Madrid, helping the Catalan club win four Champions League titles and ten La Liga titles since 2004.

Cristiano Ronaldo Cristiano Ronaldo joined Real Madrid in 2009 and went on to become one of the greatest players in the club's history. Ronaldo scored an incredible 450 goals in just 438 appearances for Real Madrid, and he played a key role in the club's three consecutive Champions League victories between 2016 and 2018. Ronaldo also played a significant role in the Real Madrid-Barcelona rivalry, scoring many important goals against Barcelona, including a hat-trick in a 3-4 win at the Camp Nou in 2014.

Memorable Matches The Real Madrid-Barcelona rivalry has produced some of the most memorable matches in football history. Here are just a few of the most iconic games:

- 1943 Copa del Rey Final: This was the first meeting between the two clubs in a major final, and Real Madrid came out on top with a 3-0 victory.

- 1960 European Cup Final: Real Madrid and Barcelona met in the final of the European Cup, with Real Madrid winning 7-3 in a thrilling match that saw Di Stefano and Puskas score four goals each.

- 2005-06 UEFA Champions League Round of 16: This was one of the most controversial matches in the rivalry's history, with Barcelona winning 2-1 after two controversial decisions went their way.

- 2010-11 La Liga: Barcelona beat Real Madrid 5-0 in a match that saw Messi score a brilliant hat-trick and cement his place as one of the greatest players of all time.

- 2013 Copa del Rey Final: Real Madrid beat Barcelona 2-1 in the final, with Ronaldo scoring.

Cultural Significance of the Rivalry in Soccer and Beyond

The rivalry between Real Madrid and Barcelona, also known as "El Clásico," is one of the most intense and longstanding in the world of soccer. The two clubs have been competing against each other for over a century, and the matches between them are always highly anticipated by fans around the globe. But the cultural significance of the rivalry goes far beyond the world of sports, and it has come to represent much more than just a simple soccer match.

The political and cultural differences between Catalonia, the region where Barcelona is located, and the rest of Spain, where Real Madrid is based, have contributed significantly to the rivalry between the two clubs. Catalonia has long been known for its separatist movement, which seeks independence from Spain, and many Barça fans see their team as a symbol of Catalan identity and pride. On the other hand, Real Madrid is often seen as a representation of Spanish nationalism and is supported by many Spaniards outside of Catalonia. As a result, the matches between the two teams have come to represent a clash of identities and values, making them much more than just a simple sporting event.

The rivalry has also had a significant impact on Spanish culture as a whole. The rivalry has been a source of inspiration for artists, writers, and musicians for decades. The matches between the two teams have been the subject of countless songs, paintings, and films, and they have helped to shape the cultural identity of both Catalonia and Spain. The rivalry has also played a significant role in the development of Spanish literature, with authors such as Manuel Vázquez Montalbán and Eduardo Mendoza using the rivalry as a backdrop for their novels.

Furthermore, the rivalry has also had a significant impact on the global soccer community. El Clásico is one of the most-watched soccer matches in the world, with millions of fans tuning in to watch the game each year. The rivalry has also helped to popularize soccer in countries where the sport was not previously popular, helping to expand the global reach of the game.

In addition, the rivalry has also had a significant economic impact. The two teams are among the most valuable sports franchises in the world, with Real Madrid consistently ranked as the most valuable soccer team in the world, according to Forbes. The rivalry between the two clubs has helped to drive ticket sales, merchandise sales, and television ratings, generating significant revenue for both teams and their respective leagues.

Overall, the cultural significance of the Real Madrid-Barcelona rivalry extends far beyond the world of sports. The rivalry has come to represent much more than just a simple soccer match, and it has helped to shape the cultural, political, and economic landscape of both Catalonia and Spain. As the rivalry continues to evolve and develop over time, it will undoubtedly continue to play a significant role in Spanish culture and in the global soccer community.

Analysis of the Teams' Playing Styles and How They Match Up Against Each Other

The rivalry between Real Madrid and Barcelona is one of the most intense and fiercely contested rivalries in world soccer. The two clubs, both based in Spain, have been battling it out on the field for over 100 years. The rivalry has transcended sport, and it is deeply ingrained in Spanish society and culture. In this section, we will analyze the teams' playing styles and how they match up against each other.

Real Madrid's Playing Style:

Real Madrid is known for their attacking style of play. They are a team that likes to take risks and are not afraid to play an expansive game. Real Madrid is blessed with some of the world's most gifted attacking players, and they like to utilize their talents to the fullest. They have a solid defensive unit that is always ready to spring into action when needed. Real Madrid's style of play is all about controlling possession, and they like to play a high-pressing game to disrupt their opponents' rhythm.

Barcelona's Playing Style:

Barcelona, on the other hand, is known for their possession-based style of play. They are a team that likes to dominate possession and control the tempo of the game. Barcelona is blessed with some of the world's most technically gifted players, and they like to utilize their talents to the fullest. They have a solid defensive unit that is always ready to spring into action when needed. Barcelona's style of play is all about controlling possession and wearing down their opponents with their constant movement and probing passes.

Matchup Analysis:

When Real Madrid and Barcelona face each other, it's a clash of two contrasting styles of play. Real Madrid likes to attack, while Barcelona likes to control possession. This has led to some incredibly exciting and high-scoring matches between the two teams over the years.

Real Madrid's attacking prowess is always a threat to Barcelona's defense, which is why Barcelona likes to control possession and limit Real Madrid's attacking opportunities. Barcelona's possession-based style of play can also be a challenge for Real Madrid's high-pressing game, as they can easily pass their way out of trouble and wear down Real Madrid's players.

One of the most crucial matchups in recent years has been between Real Madrid's Cristiano Ronaldo and Barcelona's Lionel Messi. Both players are considered two of the greatest soccer players of all time and have been the key players in their respective teams. Ronaldo's explosive speed and powerful shots are a constant threat to Barcelona's defense, while Messi's incredible dribbling skills and vision make him almost impossible to mark.

Conclusion:

Real Madrid and Barcelona's rivalry is not just about two soccer teams battling it out on the field. It is a rivalry that has transcended sport and has become a part of Spanish culture and society. The rivalry between the two clubs has given birth to some of the greatest soccer matches in history, and it has produced some of the greatest players of all time.

When Real Madrid and Barcelona face each other, it's a clash of two contrasting styles of play. Real Madrid likes to attack, while Barcelona likes to control possession. This makes for some incredibly exciting and high-scoring matches between the two teams. The rivalry between Real Madrid and Barcelona shows no signs of slowing down, and it will continue to be one of the most fiercely contested rivalries in world soccer.

Recent Matchups and Future Prospects for the Rivalry and Both Teams

Real Madrid and Barcelona have been the dominant forces in Spanish football for decades, and their intense rivalry has produced some of the most memorable matches in the history of the sport. In recent years, both teams have faced significant challenges on and off the pitch, and their rivalry has evolved in response to these changing circumstances. This section will explore the recent matchups and future prospects for the rivalry and both teams.

Recent Matchups

In recent years, the balance of power in the rivalry has shifted back and forth between Real Madrid and Barcelona. Between 2011 and 2018, Barcelona won five La Liga titles and reached the Champions League final four times, winning the competition three times. During this period, Real Madrid won just two La Liga titles and two Champions League titles, but both of those Champions League victories came against Barcelona in the semi-finals. These matches were fiercely contested and featured some of the biggest stars in world football, including Cristiano Ronaldo, Lionel Messi, and Neymar.

Since 2018, Real Madrid has reasserted itself in the rivalry, winning two consecutive La Liga titles and reaching the semi-finals of the Champions League twice. Barcelona, on the other hand, has struggled to maintain its dominance, finishing third in La Liga in the 2019-20 season and losing heavily to Bayern Munich in the quarter-finals of the Champions League. In recent matches between the two teams, Real Madrid has been the stronger side, winning the last three Clasicos (the name given to matches between Real Madrid and Barcelona) and scoring nine goals in the process.

Future Prospects

Looking ahead, the rivalry between Real Madrid and Barcelona is likely to continue to be one of the defining features of Spanish football. Both teams have ambitious plans for the future, and there are many reasons to believe that the rivalry will continue to produce some of the most exciting matches in world football.

Real Madrid is currently led by French coach Zinedine Zidane, who has won three Champions League titles with the club as both a player and a manager. The team's current squad features some of the most talented players in the world, including Sergio Ramos, Karim Benzema, and Eden Hazard. With Zidane at the helm and a talented squad at his disposal, Real Madrid is well-positioned to continue to challenge for La Liga and Champions League titles in the years to come.

Barcelona, meanwhile, has recently undergone significant changes on and off the pitch. The team's long-serving president, Josep Maria Bartomeu, resigned in 2020 following a period of unrest among the club's supporters. The team is now led by Joan Laporta, who served as president of the club from 2003 to 2010 and oversaw some of the team's most successful periods. On the pitch, Barcelona is currently led by Lionel Messi, widely regarded as one of the greatest footballers of all time. The team also features a number of talented young players, including Ansu Fati and Pedri, who are seen as the future of the club.

There are many factors that will shape the future of the rivalry between Real Madrid and Barcelona. One of the most significant is the ongoing COVID-19 pandemic, which has had a major impact on the finances of both clubs. Both teams have had to reduce their spending on transfers and salaries, and it remains to be seen how this will affect their performances on the pitch. Another factor is the changing landscape of European football, with new competitions such as the Europa Conference League set to launch in the coming years. Real Madrid and Barcelona will need to adapt to these changes if they are to continue to compete at the highest level.

Conclusion

The rivalry between Real Madrid and Barcelona is one of the most intense and storied rivalries in all of sports. The teams have played each other over 240 times, with both sides claiming victories and bitter losses. The two clubs are not just rivals on the field, but they represent different regions, languages, and cultures in Spain. The rivalry has become deeply ingrained in the social fabric of Spain, and it is hard to separate the two teams from the larger political and cultural context in which they operate. As such, the rivalry transcends soccer and has become a symbol of national identity, pride, and competition.

Looking ahead to the future of the rivalry, both Real Madrid and Barcelona will continue to be dominant forces in Spanish soccer. However, they will face new challenges in the form of other up-and-coming teams and players who are eager to challenge their dominance. In recent years, teams like Atletico Madrid and Sevilla have emerged as strong competitors in La Liga, and it remains to be seen if they will become long-term challengers to the Real Madrid-Barcelona duopoly. Additionally, both Real Madrid and Barcelona are facing significant financial challenges, and it is unclear how these will impact their ability to compete in the future.

Despite these challenges, it is certain that the rivalry between Real Madrid and Barcelona will continue to be one of the most closely-watched and anticipated matchups in the world of soccer. As long as these two teams continue to field top talent and compete at the highest level, fans will flock to stadiums and television screens to witness the latest chapter in this epic saga. Ultimately, it is the fans who will keep the rivalry alive and thriving, as they continue to invest their time, energy, and passion into supporting their favorite teams and players.

Conclusion
Recap of the Importance and Significance of Red War Rivalries in Sports

Red War Rivalries in sports are more than just games; they are cultural phenomena that bring together nations, communities, and fans from all walks of life. These rivalries transcend the sport and become symbols of cultural identity, pride, and even political tensions. The Boston Celtics vs. Los Angeles Lakers in basketball, Australia vs. England in cricket, and Real Madrid vs. Barcelona in soccer are just a few examples of Red War Rivalries that have stood the test of time and continue to captivate audiences around the world. In this chapter, we have explored the origins and development of these rivalries, the key players and memorable moments that have shaped them, their cultural significance, analysis of the teams' playing styles, and recent matchups and future prospects. Through this journey, we have gained a deeper understanding of the importance and significance of Red War Rivalries in sports.

One of the main takeaways from our exploration of Red War Rivalries is the power of sports to bring people together, create common ground, and foster a sense of community and belonging. Whether you are a fan of the Boston Celtics, the Los Angeles Lakers, the Australian cricket team, the English cricket team, Real Madrid, or Barcelona, there is a sense of shared identity and belonging that comes with supporting a team. This sense of belonging is amplified when the team represents something bigger than just themselves, such as a cultural identity, national pride, or political tensions.

Another key takeaway is the role of history in shaping Red War Rivalries. The rivalries we have explored in this chapter did not emerge overnight; they were the product of decades, if not centuries, of historical events, cultural differences, and political tensions. Understanding the historical context of these rivalries can help us appreciate them better, but also recognize the complexities that come with them.

Furthermore, the analysis of the teams' playing styles and how they match up against each other highlights the importance of strategy, tactics, and skill in these rivalries. Beyond the cultural significance and historical context, at the end of the day, it is the players on the field who determine the outcome of these games. Understanding the nuances of each team's playing style and how they match up against their rival can provide insights into what makes these games so competitive and captivating.

In conclusion, Red War Rivalries in sports are more than just games; they are cultural phenomena that reflect historical events, cultural differences, and political tensions. They bring people together, create a sense of shared identity and belonging, and offer a platform for individuals and communities to express their pride and passion. While these rivalries can sometimes be divisive, they can also be a source of unity, inspiration, and entertainment. As sports fans, we should celebrate the significance of these rivalries and appreciate the unique role they play in our lives and in society as a whole.

The Global Impact of Rivalries on Sports and Society

Sports rivalries are not limited to a specific region or country; they have a global impact on sports and society. While they may seem trivial, these rivalries can ignite passions and emotions that are felt far beyond the boundaries of the sports arena. They can bring people together or tear them apart, depending on the intensity of the rivalry and the level of sportsmanship displayed by both sides. In this section, we will explore the global impact of rivalries on sports and society.

Firstly, sports rivalries have the potential to transcend borders and bring people from different countries and cultures together. For instance, the Olympics is a prime example of how sports can be used to promote unity and understanding between nations. The Games bring together athletes from different countries, who compete against each other in a spirit of fair play and mutual respect. In some cases, rivalries that began on the playing field have evolved into lasting friendships that transcend national boundaries.

Secondly, sports rivalries can also have a negative impact on society. In some cases, they can lead to violence and unrest. This is particularly true in the case of football hooliganism, which has been a problem in many countries, including the UK, Italy, and Argentina. The intense passions and emotions associated with sports rivalries can sometimes spill over into the streets, leading to violent clashes between fans. This type of behavior not only harms individuals but also damages the reputation of the sport and the community as a whole.

Thirdly, sports rivalries can have a significant economic impact on society. Many sports rivalries attract large crowds of fans who are willing to pay top dollar for tickets, merchandise, and other items related to the rivalry. This can have a positive impact on local economies, as businesses in the area benefit from increased sales and tourism. For instance, the annual "El Clasico" football match between Real Madrid and Barcelona generates millions of dollars in revenue for the host city and the surrounding region.

Lastly, sports rivalries can also be a source of inspiration and motivation for individuals. Athletes who are part of a long-standing rivalry often strive to perform at their best and achieve greatness, not only for themselves but also for their team and their fans. This type of competition can push athletes to push their limits and reach new heights, which can have a positive impact on the sport and society as a whole.

In conclusion, sports rivalries are an integral part of the sporting world, with a global impact on sports and society. While they can bring people together and inspire individuals, they can also lead to negative outcomes if not managed appropriately. It is essential to promote fair play, respect, and sportsmanship in all sports rivalries to ensure that they continue to be a positive force in society.

The Future of Red War Rivalries in Sports in the Age of Technology and Globalization

Red war rivalries have been an integral part of the sports world for decades, captivating audiences with their intense competition and deep-rooted histories. However, with the rise of technology and globalization, the future of these rivalries is uncertain. In this section, we will examine the impact of technology and globalization on red war rivalries and discuss the future of these rivalries in the sports world.

One of the most significant changes brought about by technology and globalization is the increased access to sports around the world. Fans can now watch games live from anywhere in the world and keep up with their favorite teams and players in real-time through social media and other online platforms. This increased access has made it easier for fans to become invested in rivalries they may not have been exposed to in the past, creating new opportunities for red war rivalries to thrive.

However, technology and globalization have also created challenges for red war rivalries. The increased availability of sports around the world has led to a more diverse fan base, which can dilute the intensity of some rivalries. Additionally, the commercialization of sports has led to increased player movement, with players switching teams more frequently than in the past. This can lead to a weakening of rivalries as players move between teams that were once fierce rivals.

Another challenge brought about by technology and globalization is the potential for rivalries to become more hostile and divisive. Social media and online platforms have made it easier for fans to engage in hostile behavior and make derogatory comments about opposing teams and players. This can create a toxic environment that detracts from the spirit of healthy competition that red war rivalries are meant to embody.

Despite these challenges, red war rivalries are likely to continue to thrive in the age of technology and globalization. As long as there are passionate fans and deep-rooted histories between teams, these rivalries will continue to capture the imaginations of sports enthusiasts around the world. However, it is essential to ensure that these rivalries remain healthy and constructive, promoting healthy competition rather than divisive behavior.

In conclusion, red war rivalries are an essential part of the sports world and have played a significant role in shaping the way we think about sports and competition. The impact of technology and globalization on these rivalries is both positive and negative, creating new opportunities while also posing new challenges. Moving forward, it is essential to promote healthy competition and ensure that these rivalries continue to embody the spirit of sportsmanship and fair play that has made them so beloved around the world.

Lessons Learned from the Red War Rivalries and Their Impact on Athletes, Teams, and Fans

The Red War Rivalries in sports have provided a wealth of lessons that can be applied not only to the athletic world but also to society as a whole. Perhaps the most obvious lesson is the power of competition to bring out the best in athletes and teams. The intense rivalry between two opposing sides can push athletes to new heights of skill and achievement. The constant drive to outdo one another can lead to innovation and creativity, as athletes and teams seek new ways to gain an edge over their opponents.

Another key lesson that can be learned from Red War Rivalries is the importance of sportsmanship and respect. While the competition may be fierce on the field or court, it is important for athletes and fans alike to remember that at the end of the day, the game is just that – a game. Treating opponents with respect and dignity, regardless of the outcome of the match, is crucial in maintaining the integrity of the sport and fostering a positive environment for all involved.

The Red War Rivalries have also demonstrated the impact that sports can have on society as a whole. These intense competitions have the power to bring people together, uniting fans from around the world behind their respective teams. The sense of camaraderie and community that arises from supporting a team can be a powerful force, and can lead to lasting friendships and even social change.

One of the most important lessons to be learned from the Red War Rivalries is the importance of perseverance and resilience in the face of adversity. No matter how strong a team or athlete may be, there are always setbacks and obstacles that must be overcome. The ability to bounce back from defeat, to learn from mistakes, and to continue striving towards one's goals is a hallmark of a successful athlete, team, and person.

Finally, the Red War Rivalries have highlighted the importance of passion and dedication in achieving success. The athletes and teams that rise to the top of their respective sports do so not just through physical talent, but through a deep-seated passion for their sport and an unwavering dedication to improving their skills and achieving their goals. This dedication and passion can be applied to all areas of life, and serves as a powerful reminder that with hard work and perseverance, anything is possible.

In conclusion, the Red War Rivalries in sports have provided a rich tapestry of lessons and insights that can be applied not just to athletics, but to all areas of life. Whether it is the importance of competition, sportsmanship, community, perseverance, or passion, these rivalries have shown us what it truly means to be a successful athlete, team, and person. As we look to the future of sports in the age of technology and globalization, it is important to remember these lessons and apply them to our own lives, both on and off the field.

Final Thoughts on the Future of Red War Rivalries in Sports

As we have explored throughout this book, red war rivalries in sports have a rich history and an enduring impact on athletes, teams, and fans. From the intensity of the Boston Celtics vs. Los Angeles Lakers in basketball to the global significance of Real Madrid vs. Barcelona in soccer, these rivalries have transcended the playing field to become cultural touchstones and symbols of identity for millions around the world.

As we look to the future, there are both challenges and opportunities ahead for red war rivalries in the age of technology and globalization. On the one hand, new forms of media and communication have made it easier than ever for fans to connect with their favorite teams and players, to follow matches in real-time from anywhere in the world, and to participate in a global community of sports enthusiasts. At the same time, these same technologies have also made it easier for rivalries to become more intense and polarized, with fans on opposing sides using social media and other platforms to engage in often vitriolic exchanges that can escalate into violence and other forms of conflict.

Despite these challenges, however, there is reason to be optimistic about the future of red war rivalries in sports.

As we have seen throughout history, these rivalries have the power to inspire and unite people across geographic, cultural, and political boundaries, creating a sense of belonging and identity that transcends individual differences. Moreover, as athletes, teams, and fans continue to innovate and adapt to changing circumstances, we can expect these rivalries to evolve in new and exciting ways, incorporating new technologies, styles of play, and cultural influences to remain relevant and engaging for generations to come.

In the end, the true value of red war rivalries in sports lies not only in their ability to entertain us, but also in their ability to teach us important lessons about perseverance, dedication, and the power of competition to inspire us to be our best selves. Whether we are athletes, fans, or simply spectators, we can all learn from the examples set by the great rivalries of the past and present, and use these lessons to become better, more engaged members of the global community of sports enthusiasts.

THE END

Key Terms and Definitions

To help you better understand the language and concepts related to aging and older adults, below you will find a list of key terms and their definitions.

1. Rivalry: a competition or contest between two individuals, teams, or groups, often fueled by a desire to be superior to the other.

2. Red War Rivalries: intense and long-standing sports rivalries between two teams, often marked by hostility, aggression, and passionate fan bases.

3. Fan Culture: the attitudes, behaviors, and practices of fans of a particular sport, team, or player, including rituals, traditions, and loyalty.

4. Identity: the characteristics, beliefs, and values that define an individual, team, or group, often shaped by cultural, social, and historical factors.

5. Nationalism: a strong sense of loyalty and devotion to one's nation or country, often expressed through cultural, political, and social means.

6. Globalization: the interconnectedness and integration of countries and cultures, facilitated by technology, communication, and trade.

7. Technological Advancements: innovations and improvements in technology that have impacted sports and

sports culture, such as video replay, social media, and virtual reality.

8. Sportsmanship: the ethical and moral principles of fair play, respect, and integrity in sports, including respect for opponents and officials, adherence to rules and regulations, and acceptance of outcomes.

9. Media Coverage: the presentation and dissemination of sports-related information, news, and commentary through various media channels, including television, radio, print, and digital platforms.

10. Commercialization: the process by which sports are turned into a commodity, with economic value and profit-making potential, often involving sponsorship, advertising, merchandising, and branding.

Supporting Materials

Introduction:

- Aisenberg, A. (2017). The Evolution of Sports Fandom. In L. Wenner (Ed.), Media, Sports, and Society (pp. 243-260). SAGE Publications.
- Kram, M. (2019, November 7). The Psychology Behind Sports Rivalries. The Atlantic. https://www.theatlantic.com/health/archive/2019/11/psychology-behind-sports-rivalries/601849/
- Pope, B. (2017). Sports Rivalries: A Sociological Study. Routledge.

Chapter 1: Serena Williams vs. Maria Sharapova in Tennis

- Bodenhamer, B., & Prioreschi, P. (2017). Serena Williams vs. Maria Sharapova: Understanding Rivalry in Tennis. The Sport Journal, 20(2).
- Epstein, D. (2016). The meaning of Serena Williams. The Atlantic, 318(1), 76-85.
- Stone, J. (2019). Unbreakable: The Woman Who Defied the Nazis in the World's Most Dangerous Horse Race. Scribner.

Chapter 2: Boston Celtics vs. Los Angeles Lakers in Basketball

- Goudsmit, J. (2017). When Boston Was the Basketball Capital of the World: How the Celtics and Bruins Dominated Sports in the 1960s. University Press of New England.

- Pearlman, J. (2014). Showtime: Magic, Kareem, Riley, and the Los Angeles Lakers Dynasty of the 1980s. Gotham Books.
- Taylor, T. D. (2010). The Rivalry: Bill Russell, Wilt Chamberlain, and the Golden Age of Basketball. Random House.

Chapter 3: Australia vs. England in Cricket
- Haigh, G. (2018). Crossing the Line: How Australian Cricket Lost Its Way. Simon & Schuster Australia.
- James, T. (2019). The Cricket War: The Story of Kerry Packer's World Series Cricket. Yellow Jersey Press.
- Whimpress, B. (2019). Passage to England: Australian Cricket Tour of England 2019. Australia 2019 Ashes Series.

Chapter 4: Real Madrid vs. Barcelona in Soccer
- Balague, G. (2013). Messi. Orion Books.
- Lowe, S. (2013). Fear and Loathing in La Liga: Barcelona vs Real Madrid. Yellow Jersey Press.
- Wilson, J. (2012). Inverting the Pyramid: The History of Football Tactics. Nation Books.

Conclusion:
- Cashmore, E. (2018). Rivals: On the Psychology of Rivalry. Cambridge University Press.
- Gubar, S. (2017). Surfing the Edge of Chaos: The Laws of Nature and the New Laws of Business. Basic Books.

- Novick, A. (Director). (2017). The Vietnam War [TV Series]. PBS.

- Sennett, R. (2012). Together: The Rituals, Pleasures, and Politics of Cooperation. Yale University Press.

www.ingramcontent.com/pod-product-compliance
Lightning Source LLC
LaVergne TN
LVHW012125070526
838202LV00056B/5856